My Boss

First published 2020 by The Hedgehog Poetry Press

Published in the UK by
The Hedgehog Poetry Press
5, Coppack House
Churchill Avenue
Clevedon
BS21 6QW

www.hedgehogpress.co.uk

ISBN: 978-1-913499-39-6

9 8 7 6 5 4 3 2 1

A CIP Catalogue record for this book is available from the British Library.

My Boss

by

Niall M Oliver

MY BOSS...

never wears a belt with his green suit.
I think perhaps he is stuck
on its best colour match,

because like me, he can't decide
on the exact shade of his polyester—
army or cow pat green?

And whilst it's difficult to picture him
charging from the front line,
the idea of my boss being plopped

from the back end of a bovine
processes much easier,
and feeling relieved to be shot of him,

comes the image of the cow:
a broad smile forming
on its long face.

MY BOSS...

informs me,
his anniversary gift from his current wife is:
a vegetable tanned, 100% shell cordovan,
pedigree English calf-skin lined,
multi-compartment one of a kind
with personalised titanium buckle,
and more hand stitches than
the Bayeux Tapestry,
briefcase.

Or,
when complimented
by the new female intern:
What, that old thing?

MY BOSS...

hisses when he speaks:
Pressure! Pressure!
As if he's sprung a leak.

And here he comes again
slinking towards my desk
like a polyester snake,

a slug-shaped one
with a chip on his feeler.

MY BOSS...

says he is a born businessman
and will die a businessgod.
We appeal to the almighty:

time-off, safe conditions, equal pay.
He refuses our plea for an AC unit;
is certain the weather will turn any minute.

I imagine the sun, waiting in line
outside his office, behind the moon
and its trade union rep.

MY BOSS

I wonder those times when he dishes
out praise: *It's not bad* and *I've seen worse,*
if I'm being too harsh. Isn't it he
who pays the bills for the house I rarely see?

And that walking in his shoes
and green suit for a day
down the steep steps of a bar chart
with more red than a meat shop

might instigate my inner alpha too.
I might find a way I like my coffee served
that no other *effing* way will *effing* do.
And with glare of eye and sleight of hand,

would I delegate and motivate; wrap
the shoulder with a heavy arm,
to ensure the shit doesn't hit the fan?
Don't forget who hired you, young man.

MY BOSS

Having been caught fiddling
with the book-keeper; his beltless
green trousers by his ankles
as if halfway through shedding his skin,

comes the moment I've been waiting for
as my boss finally turns mentor—
The best advice I'll ever give you son
never shit on your own doorstep.

MY BOSS...

spins the rolodex on his desk;
It's not what you know, it's who!

I imagine someone somewhere,
any minute now, staring

considerably longer than normal
at the name blinking on their screen.

MY BOSS...

couldn't have shocked me any more
than at the church
the morning his father was buried,

when I shook his hand,
said I was sorry for his loss,
he thanked me, held my grip firm

and pulled me in close.

MY BOSS...

has inherited seven acres,
ten chickens, twelve sheep
and a flat cap—

it could be argued
this makes him no more of a farmer
than the green suit

makes him a snake. I recently learned
the sea cucumber
possesses neither heart nor balls.

MY BOSS

News of his new-found cap
has spread through the office like malware.
Rumours of early-retirement have grown hind legs.
Wagers have been placed.

A brief company memo confirms:
the cap does not fit.

Peers are despondent. Hopes have been axed.
Some have careered to job sites.
Others retrieve their hats from the ring.
I have eaten mine.

MY BOSS...

networks most evenings
at McGinnity's pub, and on weekends
at the nineteenth hole. I imagine his wife
at home on the chaise lounge

beside herself on chamomile, googling
word pairs like divorce & lawyer,
accidental & death,
basket & pungi.

MY BOSS...

has a suitable nickname.
I curse it when my alarm clock stamps its feet
to his schedule.
I mumble it when rumbling over speed bumps
on my way to work.
It festers under my coffee breath
when I pass his office.
When he talks, I can hardly hear his words
for the racket it makes in my head.
But I never write it down. Not on sticky post-it notes
or emails.
Definitely not in poems.